Credo: I Believe
Activity Book

Credo: I Believe
Activity Book

Faith and Life Series
Third Edition

BOOK FIVE

Ignatius Press, San Francisco
Catholics United for the Faith, Steubenville, Ohio

Director of First Edition: The late Rev. Msgr. Eugene Kevane, Ph.D.
Assistant Director and General Editor of First Edition: Patricia Puccetti Donahoe, M.A.
First Edition Writer: Mary Elizabeth Podhaizer

Revision Writer: Colette Ellis, M.A.
Revision Editor: Caroline Avakoff, M.A.
Revision Artist: Christopher J. Pelicano

Contents

Dear Student,

As you learn the Faith during this school year, you will read from the *Faith and Life* student text. The focus of this book is on God and his Church as understood through the Creed we profess. You will review and enter more deeply into the truths learned through the Old Testament, the life of Christ, and the beginning of the Church. Your teacher will help you to understand what you read.

This activity book is an opportunity for you to think about what you have learned each week. You will find various activities to help in this task. As you work on these activities in class or at home, you should think about what you read and discussed in class. Take the time to pray before and after the activities. Be sure to ask your teacher or your parents any questions you have.

We hope these activities and the readings from each week will help you to come to know Jesus Christ and to respond to his call to holiness.

Name:_____

God Exists

Answer the following questions in complete sentences.

1. How do we know that God exists? ʌ

God gives us faith To believne them

2. How do we encounter the revelation of God through Christ?

3. What are the truths revealed by God?

4. What is a mystery?

5. What are the two chief mysteries of our Faith that we profess in the Creed?

Name:_____

The Gift of Faith

Answer the following questions in complete sentences.

1. When did you receive the gift of faith?

2. Why don't many people have the gift of faith?

3. What things might try to lead you away from your faith?

4. How can you keep your faith strong?

5. What is a profession of faith?

6. In what do you profess belief? What prayer explains our Faith?

Name:_____

The Apostles' Creed

Write your own answers to the following questions about the Apostles' Creed.

I believe in God, the Father almighty, Creator of heaven and earth,

How is God our Father?

What does "almighty" mean?

What does "create" mean?

What does "heaven and earth" mean?

and in Jesus Christ, his only Son, our Lord, who was conceived by the Holy Spirit, born of the Virgin Mary,

Who is Jesus Christ?

How is Jesus the Son of God?

What does "Lord" mean?

If Jesus is God, and the Father is God, how can we believe in one God?

Who is the Virgin Mary?

suffered under Pontius Pilate, was crucified, died, and was buried; he descended into hell;

Who is Pontius Pilate?

Why was Jesus Crucified?

Why did Jesus descend into hell?

How long was Jesus' body buried?

Name:_____

The Apostles' Creed

Write your own answers to the following questions about the Apostles' Creed.

on the third day he rose again from the dead; he ascended into heaven, and is seated at the right hand of God the Father almighty; from there he will come to judge the living and the dead.

What happened three days after the Crucifixion of Jesus?

When did Jesus ascend into heaven?

When will Jesus come again and what will he do?

I believe in the Holy Spirit, the holy catholic Church, the communion of saints, the forgiveness of sins, the resurrection of the body, and life everlasting. Amen.

Who is the Holy Spirit?

Who founded the Catholic Church?

Who belongs to the Communion of Saints?

Who forgives sin? How can our sins be forgiven?

When will our bodies be resurrected?

What does "life everlasting" mean?

Where might a soul go after its bodily death?

What does "Amen" mean?

What prayer summarizes the chief mysteries of our Faith?

Name:_____

The Doctrines of the Creed

Across

2. He descended into _____.
5. God, the Father almighty, _____ of heaven and earth.
7. The _____ by the Holy Spirit.
9. I believe in Jesus' death and _____.
11. He ascended into heaven in _____.
12. His _____, death, and Resurrection.
13. I believe in Jesus Christ, his only _____.
14. I believe in the _____ of sins.

Down

1. I believe in the _____ of the body.
3. I believe in the holy Catholic _____.
4. He was born of the _____ _____.
6. I believe in the _____ of the living and the dead.
8. I believe in life _____.
10. He was conceived by the _____ _____.
13. I believe in the Communion of _____.

This page intentionally left blank.

Name:_____

Knowing God from the World Around Us

Answer the following questions in complete sentences.

1. Can we know that God exists without faith?

2. Name some things in God's creation that show that it had to come from someone intelligent.

3. Since most things cannot think for themselves, who guides them? (Hint: someone intelligent.)

4. Does this "someone intelligent" direct everything according to his plan?

Name:_____

God is...

Find the following words in the puzzle below. Note: these words may be spelled backwards or diagonally!

Supreme	All Wise	Loving	Merciful
Omniscient	Almighty	Kind	Generous
Eternal	All Present	Tenderhearted	Gentle
All Powerful	All Good	All Perfect	Immense
All Holy	Majestic	Spirit	

```
A T N E I C S I N M O W D H T A T S A I A
Y A T F T E R Y O U T F N E S E R P L L A
I M M E N S E H P N L E I A S E P R L A L
I Y F O N M E I E N M E K D I T G P G R E
L A T L Y D O S N L Y E G N I V O L O M G
E W S U P R E M E I L L R E L W L W O E A
T T A N I R R E T S P O C E S I B N L E
A R E L P L Y T H I E S A R I U J T P U Z
N A L L C O O D S E L R F E D F L U O N O
O A L T A G R E E W A U N I T E U E N E X
I A T W E W I L L R L R E A V Y L L H L A
S V I E W D O O G L L A T H L O W T O L O
S P K U P S A P A L W E C E I F I S L C S
A Y L O H L L A A K I O O P D S I P M I U
P I B L E Q M A J E S T I C U O E I T E O
M S E D A L I N E E E A F T E R E R T H R
O T W E W I G L T A L C A B F O U I T C E
C E A T I O H N U T W H Y E G O O T C R N
C A T E D Y T O U O F A C L L P E O Q L E
E T O K N O Y W L O V T E A N D S E R V G
```

Name:_____

The Blessed Trinity

Answer the following questions in complete sentences.

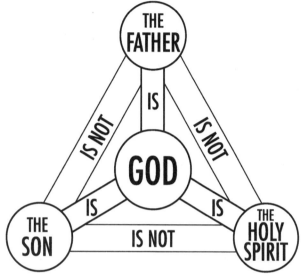

1. What is the Blessed Trinity?

2. How many gods do we believe in?

3. How many Persons are in God?

4. Is one Person more powerful/wise/better than the others?

5. What is the nature of the Father? of the Son? of the Holy Spirit?

6. Can we fully understand the Blessed Trinity? Why?

Name:_____

Mystery of God

Answer the following questions in complete sentences.

1. What does the "Unity of God" mean?

2. What does "Blessed Trinity" mean?

3. What does it mean to say that the three Divine Persons are "distinct" from one another?

4. Who is the First Person of the Blessed Trinity? Why?

5. Who is the Second Person of the Blessed Trinity? Why?

6. Who is the Third Person of the Blessed Trinity? Why?

7. Is each Divine Person of the Blessed Trinity God?

8. Are the three Divine Persons equal?

Name:_____

Creation

Add to this picture in blue some things God creates and in red some things man makes.

Name:_____

Thanking God for Creation

What are some things God created that you are thankful for?

Name:_____

Creator of Heaven and Earth

Answer the following questions in complete sentences.

1. Explain what it means to create and why only God can be called the Creator.

2. Explain how God cares for his creation.

From observing creation we can learn a little about what God is. We can know that he exists, that he is powerful, wise, and good. Give examples of things present in the world today that show us these truths about God and how he cares for his creation.

1. God exists:

2. God is all powerful:

3. God is all wise:

4. God is all good:

Name:_____

Learning About God from His Creation

Answer the following questions in complete sentences.

1. How do we know that God is not created?

2. Why did God make heaven and earth?

3. Did the universe make itself? How do you know?

4. What can we learn from the way plants, animals, and weather all seem to work together in harmony?

5. Should we stop to admire God's creation?

6. Does God know the big and little things?

7. What must we do to show God that we are thankful for his creation? Can you think of some examples?

Name:_____

Angels

Answer the following questions in complete sentences.

1. What is an angel? Is it a creature?

2. Are all the angels the same?

3. Can we see angels? Why?

4. What are some different choirs or orders of angels?

5. Are angels intelligent?

Name:_____

God Tests the Angels

Explain what happened after God created the angels. What happened when God tested the angels? What happened to them? What do the angels do now?

Name:_____

Realm of the Angels

The word angel means "messenger." In the Bible we often find angels acting as God's messengers, bringing to people news of God's plan for them. Read the following passages from both the Old and New Testaments, and then state what message the angel was bringing.

Genesis 22:1–19

Judges 13:1–14

Tobit 5:1–6 and Tobit 12

Luke 1:5–23

Luke 1:26–38

Luke 2:8–20

Matthew 2:13–23

Acts 12:1–11

Name:_____

Angels: God's Messengers

Answer the following questions in complete sentences.

1. What are pure spirits?

2. How do we know that pure spirits exist?

3. What creatures that are pure spirits do we know through faith?

4. What are the angels?

5. Do we have duties toward the angels?

6. What are demons?

7. Can you think of different angels in the Bible? When do we hear about angels?

Name:_____

Made in His Image

Read Genesis 1:26–27, and then tell what it means that man is made in the image and likeness of God.

There are various levels of life or existence in God's creation. There is a certain order or hierarchy among them.

SPIRITUAL
Divine Life
Angelic Life
Human Life*
MATERIAL
Human Life*
Animal Life (sensitive)
Plant Life (vegetative)
Non-life (inanimate)

Man shares in both the spiritual and material life because he is composed of both body and soul. See if you can give an example of what men have in common with the following groups:

Angelic:

Animal:

Vegetative:

Name:_____

Man Before the Fall

Before the Fall, man had all he needed to be happy. He would not be sick, he would not suffer, and he would not even die! Draw a picture of the Garden of Eden.

Name:_____

Called to Heaven

Answer the following questions in complete sentences.

1. What supernatural gift did Adam and Eve possess before the Fall?

2. What other gifts did Adam and Eve possess before the Fall?

3. Adam and Eve were blessed by God's presence. They had a special relationship with God. Were we all to receive this gift? Are we now? How?

Name:_____

God Made Man in His Image

Answer the following questions in complete sentences.

1. What does it mean to be made in the image and likeness of God? Does God have a body?

2. Who is made in the image of God? Old people? Young people? Unborn babies?

3. Why is man a special creature? What two worlds does he share in?

4. What was life like for Adam and Eve before Original Sin?

5. Does God know and love each and every one of us as his children?

Name:_____

You Shall Be Like Gods!

Answer the following questions in complete sentences.

1. Did Adam and Eve know God's love?

2. What was the test God had for Adam and Eve?

3. Why was eating a piece of fruit so serious?

4. Whom did Adam and Eve choose to follow?

5. What were Adam and Eve like after they had eaten the fruit?

Name:_____

Before and After the Fall

Compare the two columns and reflect on life before and after the Fall.

Before the Fall

1. Adam and Eve had God's life in them.

2. Adam and Eve did not know evil, pain, or suffering.

3. Before the Fall, Adam and Eve did not have to labor.

4. They did not have to die.

5. They lived in the Garden of Eden.

After the Fall

1. Adam and Eve no longer had God's life and could not go to heaven.

2. After the Fall, they were sad and knew evil. They also suffered.

3. After the Fall, they had to work very hard, even for food.

4. They would die and their bodies would return to dust.

5. They had to leave the Garden of Eden and needed a Savior in order to go to heaven.

Name: _____

Jesus Christ, the New Adam

The New Adam, Jesus Christ, passed the test for all of us. He died on the Cross in order to bring us new life through Baptism. Reflect on Jesus as the New Adam by using the pictures below.

Name:_____

The Fall from Grace

Because of his sin Adam lost God's friendship and special gifts. Fill in the chart below by describing Adam and Eve before and after their fall from grace.

Before the Fall	After the Fall

Sin not only affects men, but also the world around us. Compare the world before and after the Fall.

Before the Fall	After the Fall

Why does God allow suffering to exist?

Name:_____

Abraham, Sarah, and Isaac

Answer the following questions in complete sentences.

1. What was the first thing God asked of Abraham?

2. What did Abraham do in faith?

3. What did God promise to Abraham? Did Abraham believe him?

4. How did God reward Abraham?

5. Give two reasons we can call Abraham our father in faith.

Name:_____

God Will Provide a Lamb!

In a few sentences, describe how the sacrifice of Isaac foreshadows God's sacrifice of his own Son, Jesus Christ.

Name:_____

Isaac

Answer the following questions in complete sentences.

1. When Isaac grew up, whom did he marry?

2. Did they have children?

3. What prophecy did Rebecca receive?

4. How did Jacob trick Esau?

5. What is a birthright? Why was it wrong for Esau to sell it?

6. What is the importance of the blessing? Why would Esau be mad that Jacob received this from Isaac?

7. Why did Jacob leave?

Name:_____

God's Chosen People in Egypt

Reflect upon the life of Joseph in Egypt.

Jacob had a special love for Joseph, and this made Joseph's brothers jealous. On top of that, Joseph had special dreams saying his brothers would bow down before him. His brothers came to hate him, so they sold him into slavery in Egypt. Joseph became the governor of Egypt and saved Egypt from a famine. Joseph's brothers, however, were afflicted by the famine and came to buy grain from Joseph. Without recognizing Joseph, they bowed down before him. Joseph had forgiven his brothers, and invited his whole family to come and live in Egypt. They grew in number rapidly and soon became feared by the Egyptians who worshipped different gods.

Name:_____

I Am Has Sent You

Answer the following questions in complete sentences.

1. How did God speak to Moses?

2. What did God want of Moses?

3. Did Moses respond with faith? Was he obedient?

4. Who would help Moses?

5. What would Aaron do?

Name:_____

Plagues: Getting Pharaoh's Attention

Number the plagues in the order in which they occurred.

_____ Frogs

_____ Blood

_____ Locusts

_____ Boils

_____ Flies

_____ Hail

_____ Darkness

_____ Death of firstborn

_____ Death of cattle

_____ Gnats

Name:_____

Passover

Answer the following questions in complete sentences.

1. From what plague did the Passover save the Israelites?

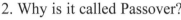

2. Why is it called Passover?

3. What did each family have to do?

4. A lamb was to be sacrificed and eaten. What Sacrament did this foretell?

5. Why were they to eat dressed for travel?

6. When did the Israelites leave?

7. Were they safe now?

Name:_____

Preparing for Salvation

Answer the following questions.

Prefigurement

1. The Israelites were slaves to Pharaoh.

2. Israel needed God to save them.

3. A lamb was sacrificed at Passover.

4. The Israelites ate the Passover lamb.

5. The blood of the lamb was put on the doorposts and saved them from the angel of death.

6. The Israelites crossed the Red Sea on the way home to the Promised Land.

7. The Israelites received God's law.

8. Pharaoh's army was destroyed.

9. God made a covenant with Israel.

Fulfillment in Our Salvation

1. To whom were we slaves? (in our sin)

2. How did God save us?

3. Who was sacrificed for us?

4. What Sacrament nourishes us and is the Paschal Lamb?

5. Whose blood was shed on the Cross, saving us from death, and opening heaven for us?

6. Our Promised Land is heaven. What Sacrament do we receive to start our journey?

7. Do we follow God's law? Who taught it perfectly?

8. What is destroyed in our Baptism?

9. How did God make the perfect covenant with us?

Name:_____

God Cares for His People

Answer the following questions in complete sentences.

1. How did the people behave in the desert?

2. How did God care for them?

3. Why did God set apart these people?

Name:_____

The Ten Commandments

Write out the Ten Commandments.

Faith and Life Series • Grade 5 • Chapter 9 • Lesson 2

Name:_____

The Ark of the Covenant

Answer the following questions in complete sentences.

1. Who wanted an Ark made?

2. What would the Ark hold?

3. Of what was the Ark to be a sign?

4. What was special about the Ark? Why was it so important to the Hebrews?

Name:_____

Kings of Israel

Answer the following questions in complete sentences.

1. Why did Israel start to have kings?

2. Who were two of Israel's greatest kings?

3. Why were they great kings?

4. Did God ever forget his promise that the Savior would come through these people?

Name:_____

Prophets

Answer the following questions in complete sentences.

1. What does a prophet do?

2. What sins were the Israelites committing?

3. Would they marry pagans?

4. What happened when the Israelites forgot their covenant with God?

5. What would the prophet tell them to do?

6. Were prophets popular?

7. How did the Israelites know they were wrong (when they did not want to listen to the prophets)?

Name:_____

Spread the Word

Prophets were to keep God's people from being unfaithful. They called people back to God and his truth. If you were a prophet, what message do you think God would have you deliver?

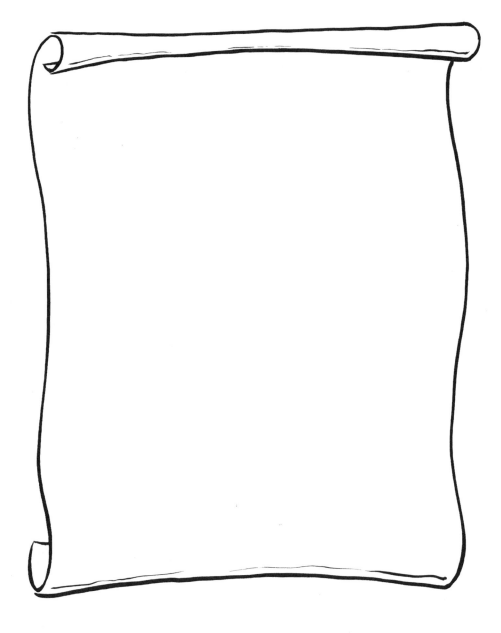

Name:_____

Isaiah

Answer the following questions in complete sentences.

1. Who was Isaiah?

2. For what was Isaiah sent to prepare the people?

3. What did Isaiah predict?

4. What were the Jewish people expecting of the Messiah?

5. How did the Messiah differ from what the Jews expected?

6. What would the Messiah suffer for us?

7. Look up the scriptural passage in Isaiah 7:14. What did Isaiah say?

8. When were Isaiah's words fulfilled?

Name:_____

Idol Worship

Answer the following questions in complete sentences.

1. Which prophets spoke against idol worship?

2. Who was worshipping idols?

3. Whose sinful actions was Jeremiah to oppose?

4. Why did idol worship displease God?

5. What commandment did this break?

6. What does this commandment say?

Name:_____

John the Baptist

Answer the following questions in complete sentences.

1. Write about the miraculous birth of John the Baptist.

2. What would John the Baptist do?

Name:_____

The Annunciation

Answer the following questions in complete sentences.

1. Write out Mary's *Magnificat* found in Luke 1:46–55.

2. What did the Angel Gabriel say to Mary?

3. How would this happen?

4. What did Mary answer?

Name:_____

The Visitation

Answer the following questions in complete sentences.

1. When did Mary go to visit her cousin Elizabeth?

2. What happened when Mary greeted Elizabeth?

3. What did Elizabeth say?

4. How long did Mary stay with Elizabeth?

Name:_____

The Immaculate Conception

Answer the following questions in complete sentences.

1. What does "Immaculate Conception" mean?

2. Why did God give Mary this gift?

3. Was Mary free from Original Sin?

4. Why do we say that Mary is full of grace?

5. What was Mary worthy to become?

6. Did Mary ever offend God?

7. When do we celebrate the Immaculate Conception?

Name:_____

Saint Joseph

Answer the following questions in complete sentences.

1. What decision did Saint Joseph have to make?

2. What did he decide?

3. What did an angel tell him?

4. How did Joseph feel about this? Why?

5. Why did they have to go to Bethlehem?

6. Was Saint Joseph the father of Jesus?

Name:_____

The Nativity

Using a Bible, read the account of the nativity from the Gospel of Luke. In your own words, describe the birth of Jesus.

Name:_____

The Incarnation

Answer the following questions in complete sentences.

1. Is Jesus God?

2. What does Incarnation mean?

3. Why did the Son of God take on humanity?

4. Did Jesus have two natures? What were they?

5. Did Jesus have human emotions?

6. Did Jesus cease being God when he was born?

7. Are there two persons in Jesus?

8. How does the Incarnation honor the human race?

Name:_____

The Presentation

Answer the following questions in complete sentences.

1. Why did Mary and Joseph take Jesus to the temple?

2. Who was filled with joy? Why?

3. How did Simeon know that Jesus was the Messiah?

4. What did Simeon call Jesus?

5. What did Simeon say to Mary?

Name:_____

The Hidden Years

Answer the following questions in complete sentences.

1. What do we call the time after the Holy Family returned from Egypt until the time of Jesus' baptism?

2. What kind of life did Jesus have with his family?

3. How did other people see Jesus?

4. Would Jesus have helped his parents?

5. Would Jesus have been obedient to his parents?

6. The Bible tells us about an event that happened when Jesus was twelve. Why did Jesus and his family go to Jerusalem?

7. What happened on the way back?

8. Where was Jesus found?

Name:_____

Mary

Answer the following questions in complete sentences.

1. Who is the Blessed Virgin Mary?

2. Was she really the Mother of Jesus?

3. Is she the Mother of God?

Name:_____

Saint Joseph

Answer the following questions in complete sentences.

1. Who is Saint Joseph?

2. Was Saint Joseph the father of Jesus?

3. How did Saint Joseph care for Jesus and Mary?

Name:_____

The Holy Family

How can you follow the example of the Holy Family? Explain these four steps and use an example from life within your own family.

1. Accept God's will for you.

2. Do the job you are meant to do in your family.

3. Make God a member of your family.

4. Do good for others as a family.

Name:_____

Christ's Baptism

Answer the following questions in complete sentences.

1. How old was Jesus when he was baptized?

2. Who baptized Jesus?

3. Who is John the Baptist?

4. Why did crowds come to see John the Baptist? What did he tell them?

5. How did John preach the coming of the Messiah?

6. Did John want to baptize Jesus? Why?

7. What happened after Jesus was baptized?

Name:_____

Jesus' Temptation

Answer the following questions in complete sentences.

1. Who tempted Jesus?

2. Where was Jesus tempted?

3. Jesus left John the Baptist and went into the desert to fast and pray for forty days. At the end of the forty days Satan came to tempt Jesus. Satan tempted Jesus three times. Draw lines to match Satan's temptation with Jesus' refusal and his response.

Satan Tempting

"If you are the Son of God, command these stones to become loaves of bread."

"If you are the Son of God, throw yourself down; for it is written, 'He will give his angels charge of you.'"

"All these [kingdoms of the world] I will give you, if you will fall down and worship me."

Jesus' Response

"You shall not tempt the Lord your God."

"You shall worship the Lord your God and him only shall you serve."

"Man shall not live by bread alone, but by every word that proceeds from the mouth of God."

4. Why did Jesus go into the desert?

5. What did Jesus do to prepare himself for his work?

Name:_____

Kingdom of God

Read the following parables from the Bible: Matthew 13:4–9, 18–23, 24–30, 31–32, 33, 44, 45–46, and 47–50. Draw a picture of the parable that best helps you to understand what the Kingdom of God is like. Then write a short paragraph describing how the parable teaches us about God's Kingdom.

Name:_____

The Apostles

Answer the following questions in complete sentences.

1. Who were the Apostles?

2. What did the Apostles do?

3. What would be the mission of the Apostles?

4. Can you name the twelve Apostles?

Name:_____

Jesus Teaches the Truth

Answer the following questions in complete sentences.

1. When did Jesus start teaching?

2. What did Jesus teach?

3. What was Jesus' mysterious news?

4. Why were the Jews not ready for this truth?

5. Why did Jesus have to reveal the truth about himself little by little?

Name:_____

Miracles

Answer the following questions in complete sentences.

1. How was Jesus Christ known to be the Son of God?

2. What is a miracle?

3. With what miracles did Jesus demonstrate that he is True God?

Can you find these words?

Transfiguration	Believe	Walk on water	Heal
Resurrection	Deaf	Simple	Health
Miracles	Speech	Son of God	Life
Exorcism	Blind	I am	Storm

```
E  M  H  O  E  X  O  R  C  I  S  M  B  S  A
M  I  E  T  R  A  S  P  E  E  C  H  L  T  E
T  R  A  N  S  F  I  G  U  R  A  T  I  O  N
W  A  L  K  O  N  W  A  T  E  R  L  N  R  E
D  C  X  H  B  E  L  I  E  V  E  M  D  M  L
E  L  H  E  A  L  T  H  R  S  I  A  M  A  I
A  E  R  E  S  U  R  R  E  C  T  I  O  N  F
F  S  O  N  O  F  G  O  D  S  I  M  P  L  E
```

Name:_____

Jesus Calms the Storm

Read Luke 8:22–25. Write about what happened as if you were there.

Jesus Christ

Circle the correct answer.

1. What was Jesus' mysterious news?
    a. he is an angel
    b. he is the Son of God
    c. he is a prophet

2. Jesus is:
    a. human
    b. divine
    c. both human and divine

3. The Jews accused Jesus of:
    a. blasphemy
    b. adultery
    c. theft

4. The Jews thought the Messiah would be:
    a. a descendant of David
    b. a holy leader
    c. both a and b

5. Jesus gave hints of his divinity through:
    a. writing a book
    b. visions
    c. miracles

6. Who were the first outside the Holy Family to learn the truth about Jesus' divinity?
    a. the Apostles
    b. the humble
    c. fishermen

7. Who did people say that Jesus was?
    a. a prophet
    b. God
    c. a magician

8. Who revealed the truth about Jesus to Peter?
    a. Mary
    b. Jesus
    c. God the Father

9. When Jesus revealed his glory on the mountain, it was called:
    a. the Transformation
    b. the Transfiguration
    c. the Translation

10. Who appeared with Jesus on the mountain?
    a. Moses
    b. Elijah
    c. Moses and Elijah

11. What name did Jesus take as his own?
    a. Jesus
    b. Son of God
    c. I AM

12. What miracle was the greatest proof of Jesus' divinity?
    a. the Transfiguration
    b. the Resurrection
    c. exorcisms

Name:_____

Forgiveness of Sins

Answer the following questions in complete sentences.

1. How did Jesus make his divinity known?

2. Over what did Jesus have authority?

3. What is so special about Jesus forgiving sins?

4. How did Jesus show that he had the power to forgive sins?

5. What two things did Jesus heal?

6. How does Jesus forgive our sins today?

Name:_____

The Prodigal Son

Read Luke 15:11–32. In your own words, describe what happened in the story of the Prodigal Son.

Name:_____

Zacchaeus

Answer the following questions in complete sentences.

1. Who is Zacchaeus?

2. How had Zacchaeus sinned?

3. How did Zacchaeus change his ways?

Name:_____

Your Sins are Forgiven

Fill in the crossword puzzle with the correct words.

Across

1. The _____ _____ is one of the parables Jesus told in order to teach us about God's love and forgiveness.
2. Some of the _____ were angry because Jesus said he could forgive sins.
3. Jesus told us how happy God is when sinners _____.

Down

4. Jesus came to give us God's _____.
5. Jesus' enemies called him the friend of tax collectors and _____.
6. Jesus wants us to have _____ for our sins.
7. _____ was a tax collector who promised to give back four times the amount of any money he had gotten dishonestly.

Name:_____

Jesus: Human and Divine

Jesus is both God and man. Below are Scripture passages, which show the human and divine life of Jesus. Mark the ones that show Jesus' divinity with a "D" and the ones that show his humanity with an "H".

_____ John 11:25–26

_____ John 7:37–39

_____ Luke 2:6–7

_____ John 6:41–53

_____ John 11:33–36

_____ Matthew 21:18

_____ Mark 1:35

_____ Mark 6:3

_____ Luke 3:22

_____ Luke 8:26–33

Name:_____

True God and True Man

List the ways Jesus showed that he is truly God and truly man.

True God	True Man

Name:_____

Jesus: My Model

Answer the following questions in complete sentences.

1. Why did God the Father send Jesus to us?

2. How did Jesus teach us?

3. How did Jesus teach us to obey?

4. How did Jesus show us to love?

5. How did Jesus show us to forgive?

6. How did Jesus show us to accept God's will?

7. How did Jesus show us to be humble?

8. Why did Jesus become man?

9. What can we share with Jesus?

10. What question can we ask if we are not sure what to do?

Name:_____

Jesus Christ

Answer the following questions in complete sentences.

1. Is Jesus God? Is Jesus Man?

2. Is Jesus a human person or a Divine Person?

3. Was God disguised as man in Jesus?

4. Did Jesus, the Son of God, exist from all eternity? As God or as man?

5. When did the Son of God take on a human nature?

6. What does human nature include?

7. Was Jesus one or two persons?

8. Did Jesus have one or two natures?

9. How do we know Jesus is God?

10. When will we fully understand the mystery of Jesus taking on human nature? What is this mystery called?

11. Can we share the events in our lives with Jesus?

12. Why would we ask, "Jesus, what would you do if this happened to you?"

Rejecting & Accepting Christ

Read the situations below. Write "R" before those that show rejection of Christ.
Write "A" before those situations that show acceptance of Christ.

Examples from the Gospels

_____ 1. Mary anointed the feet of Jesus with expensive perfume in order to express her love for him.

_____ 2. Judas betrayed Christ with a kiss.

_____ 3. The wise men came to adore the Christ Child but did not tell Herod, afterward, where the Christ Child was.

_____ 4. Herod tried to kill the Christ Child by ordering all the baby boys in his area murdered.

_____ 5. A sinful woman came into a party where Jesus was in order to wash his feet and show him proper courtesy.

_____ 6. The Pharisees and the scribes constantly sought to trap Christ.

_____ 7. Some of the Apostles were arguing who was the greatest among them.

_____ 8. While Jesus was on trial, Peter denied that he knew him.

Examples from Today

_____ 1. The Supreme Court decided in the *Roe vs. Wade* case in 1973 to make abortion legal in the United States.

_____ 2. Many Christians are working together to restore the unborn baby's right to life.

_____ 3. Jim swears, thinking he will not be accepted unless he uses God's name in vain.

_____ 4. Jane's parents will not allow her to watch TV shows in which people act as if God does not exist.

_____ 5. Mary Beth hears a group of girls making fun of a new girl. Mary Beth tells the girls to stop their gossiping.

_____ 6. John gives up a professional baseball game in order to fulfill his Sunday Mass obligation.

_____ 7. Catherine ignores her mother's request for help around the house and goes out to play with her friends.

_____ 8. Tom makes an effort to visit our Lord every day in the Blessed Sacrament.

On a separate piece of paper, write out five examples of situations of rejecting and accepting Christ.

Name:_____

Will You Stay With Jesus?

Answer the following questions in complete sentences.

If we really believe the Eucharist is the Body, Blood, Soul, and Divinity of Jesus Christ, we would make every effort to attend Mass and make visits to the Blessed Sacrament.

1. Read John 6:27–59. What does Jesus call himself?

2. Was Jesus speaking in riddles?

3. What did many people who liked Jesus do?

4. Why did they turn away?

5. Did many disciples turn away from Jesus? Why?

6. What was Jesus talking about when he said we would eat his Body and drink his Blood?

7. How do we know that the Eucharist is really and truly the Body, Blood, Soul, and Divinity of Jesus Christ?

Name:_____

The Messiah

Explain what each of the following groups expected of the Messiah and tell why they did not accept Jesus.

Pharisees

Sadducees

Scribes

Zealots

Name:_____

Turning Away from Jesus

Answer the following questions in complete sentences.

1. Was the rejection of Jesus a one-time event?

2. Who rejected Jesus and why?

3. How do we reject Jesus?

4. What happens when we commit a mortal sin?

5. What happens when we commit a venial sin?

6. Does our world today reject Jesus? How? Where?

7. How can we show Jesus that we do not reject him?

Name:_____

Accepting the Father's Will

Answer the following questions in complete sentences.

1. What happened when Jesus came into Jerusalem?

2. Were these people faithful to him?

3. Did Jesus warn his disciples what would happen to him?

4. Did they understand him? How do we know?

5. Did Jesus freely lay down his life, or was it taken from him?

6. What happened in the Garden of Gethsemane after the Last Supper?

Name:_____

The Last Supper

Answer the following questions in complete sentences.

1. What feast did Jesus and his Apostles celebrate at the Last Supper?

2. What did Jesus do to teach them a lesson in humility?

3. What did Jesus institute at the Last Supper?

4. What power did Jesus give to his Apostles?

5. When was the first Mass?

Name:_____

Thy Will be Done

Answer the following questions in complete sentences.

1. Where did Jesus take his disciples after the Last Supper?

2. Why did Jesus pray to the Father?

3. What hurt Jesus the most?

4. What happened in Jesus' sorrow and Agony in the Garden?

5. Whom did God send to comfort Jesus?

Name:_____

The Acceptance of the Father's Will

Fill in the crossword puzzle with the correct words.

The Passion of Christ took place at the time of the Jewish _____ (*7 across*).

On _____ (*7 down*) Sunday Jesus rode into Jerusalem on a donkey. The crowds waved palm branches and cried out, "_____ (*1 across*) is he who comes in the name of the _____ (*5 across*)."

On _____ (*11 down*) Thursday Jesus shared the Last _____ (*10 down*) with his Apostles. Before the meal Jesus _____ (*3 across*) the feet of the Apostles. After the meal Jesus took _____ (*8 across*) and _____ (*3 down*) and changed them into his _____ (*2 across*) and _____ (*12 down*). He gave it to the Apostles; this was their first _____ (*4 across*).

On Good _____ (*6 across*) we commemorate Christ's _____ (*13 down*) for the redemption of men. Jesus was made to carry his _____ (*9 down*). Jesus was crucified at _____ (*4 down*).

Name:_____

The Perfect Sacrifice

Look up the following accounts of sacrifices in the Old Testament and for each one answer the following: 1. Who is the priest or the one who offers the sacrifice? 2. What is the offering or victim of the sacrifice? 3. What is the reason or purpose for offering the sacrifice? 4. What is the effect or merit of the sacrifice?

Sacrifice of Abel (Genesis 4:4)

1.

2.

3.

4.

Sacrifice of Melchizedek (Genesis 14:18–20)

1.

2.

3.

4.

Sacrifice of Abraham (Genesis 22:13)

1.

2.

3.

4.

Sacrifice of the Israelites (Leviticus 1:3–9)

1.

2.

3.

4.

Name:_____

Old and New Covenants & Sacrifices

Compare the Old and New Covenants and sacrifices.

Old Testament Sacrifice & Covenant   *Jesus' Sacrifice & the New Covenant*

1. Was a lamb sacrificed?   1. Was a lamb sacrificed?

2. Was the lamb eaten?   2. Was the lamb eaten? How?

3. Did God share a   3. Did God share a covenant
   covenant with man?   with man?

4. Would this covenant   4. Would this covenant
   last forever?   last forever?

5. Would laws have to   5. Would laws have to
   be kept?   be kept?

6. Would heaven be opened?   6. Would heaven be opened?

7. Would man receive grace?   7. Would man receive grace?

8. Could everyone share in this sacrifice?   8. Could everyone share in this
                                               sacrifice? How?

Name:_____

The Sacrifice of the Mass

Answer the following questions.

1. What is the Mass?

2. Is it the same sacrifice as the one that took place 2000 years ago?

3. Who says the words of Christ?

4. How is Jesus' Body and Blood offered to God?

5. How did your priest receive this power?

6. How do we participate in the Mass?

7. What can we give Jesus during the Mass? What can he do with them?

Name:_____

Martyrs: Persecuted for the Faith

Write a letter to God offering yourself and your works as a sacrifice to God.

Blessed Kateri Tekakwitha, pray for us!

Name:_____

He is Risen!

Pretend that you are Mary Magdalene. What happened on Easter morning?

Name:_____

Jesus' Resurrection

Answer the following questions in complete sentences.

1. What did Jesus' Resurrection show all of his followers?

2. What victory had Jesus won?

3. Did God accept Jesus' sacrifice? How do we know?

4. Who was the first person to see the Resurrected Lord?

5. Who were the first Apostles to see the empty tomb?

6. What does the Bible tell us to confirm that Jesus rose from the dead?

Name:_____

Jesus' Resurrected Body

Answer the following questions in complete sentences.

1. Was Jesus' body changed after the Resurrection?

2. How was Jesus' body different from ours?

3. How was Jesus' body the same as ours?

Name:_____

He is Risen

Find the twenty words referring to the events of Jesus' Passion, death, and Resurrection. Some words are spelled backwards or diagonally.

Gardener	Guards	Easter Sunday	Angel
Mary Magdalene	John	Peter	Women
Disciple	Risen	Resurrection	Weeping
Body	Tomb	Three	Stone
Jesus	Glorified	Buried	Master

```
N  U  W  U  V  B  G  I  W  Q  U  V  M  T  Y  M  S  P
Y  O  F  F  O  S  U  H  D  T  Q  G  D  I  A  D  H  K
W  U  I  H  K  B  A  F  N  P  Z  Y  X  R  A  H  O  N
V  G  T  T  W  U  R  S  Q  O  B  G  Y  C  L  A  U  B
U  T  D  K  C  Z  D  A  X  R  S  M  T  H  R  E  E  O
L  A  E  B  P  E  S  W  P  K  A  R  E  T  S  A  M  P
K  H  W  K  Q  M  R  Y  O  G  E  L  Y  X  F  V  U  G
X  B  M  E  D  J  L  R  D  M  F  R  F  D  M  Z  E  X
O  U  W  X  E  O  C  A  U  E  E  E  K  F  A  A  H  L
D  Q  U  Y  O  P  L  S  R  S  L  N  D  G  B  C  F  X
K  M  A  V  A  E  I  N  E  P  E  W  E  W  D  D  Q  A
Q  F  B  X  N  J  R  N  I  R  G  R  I  N  H  O  J  I
I  N  T  E  Z  G  L  C  G  Y  O  M  F  X  Q  E  K  K
W  Q  Q  B  A  Z  S  M  E  E  N  J  I  I  H  V  S  B
O  Y  T  O  U  I  L  Z  U  F  R  Y  R  Q  S  E  U  B
J  L  K  P  D  J  W  D  P  I  C  X  O  U  O  R  O  S
V  Z  V  O  E  U  D  Q  S  K  N  C  L  K  I  J  J  Z
Y  A  D  N  U  S  R  E  T  S  A  E  G  E  B  E  Y  L
W  X  O  H  J  K  N  W  E  U  I  L  D  S  M  S  W  H
E  T  B  H  T  X  E  N  N  L  A  M  E  J  O  U  R  Y
S  P  Z  K  M  N  B  C  T  T  K  A  O  G  T  S  E  Y
D  G  V  L  W  O  Q  C  Y  M  Q  Z  Y  V  N  M  T  L
K  W  R  D  W  J  G  A  R  D  E  N  E  R  W  A  E  W
A  C  K  K  G  F  U  A  F  D  A  Q  T  N  C  A  P  E
U  X  G  S  P  H  Q  D  A  K  Q  T  I  G  V  P  S  N
```

Name:_____

Forgiveness of Sins

Answer the following questions in complete sentences.

1. During the days after the Resurrection of Jesus, what did Jesus do?

2. What did Jesus instruct his Apostles to do?

3. When Jesus breathed on them, what did he give them?

4. What power did the Apostles now have?

5. With this power, what could the Apostles do?

6. Who were the first priests and bishops?

7. How can we receive God's mercy and forgiveness?

Name:_____

Jesus and Peter

Answer the following questions in complete sentences.

1. Where did Jesus question Peter?

2. What did Jesus ask Peter?

3. What did Peter reply?

4. How many times did Jesus ask Peter the same question?

5. How many times had Peter denied Jesus?

6. What was Jesus' command to Peter?

7. What was Jesus doing by issuing the command to Peter?

8. What role did Jesus give to Peter?

9. Who now is Peter's successor? Does he continue Peter's mission?

Name:_____

The Ascension

Answer the following questions in complete sentences.

1. How long did Jesus stay on earth after the Resurrection?

2. What did Jesus do during that time after his Resurrection?

3. Why would Jesus leave?

4. What did Jesus promise his Apostles?

5. What command did he give to his Apostles?

6. Will Jesus leave us alone?

7. Who appeared to the Apostles? What did they say?

The Giver of Life

For the following Scripture quotes, tell who is speaking and to whom the words are addressed.

"If you forgive the sins of any, they are forgiven; if you retain the sins of any, they are retained."
Speaker:

Addressed to:

"Unless I see in his hands the print of the nails, and place my finger in the mark of the nails, and place my hand in his side, I will not believe."
Speaker:

Addressed to:

"You have believed because you have seen me. Blessed are those who have not seen and yet believe."
Speaker:

Addressed to:

"You know that I love you."
Speaker:

Addressed to:

"Feed my sheep."
Speaker:

Addressed to:

"Men of Galilee, why do you stand looking into heaven?"
Speaker:

Addressed to:

Name:_____

Come, Holy Spirit

Look up the following Scripture passages and tell what they say about the Holy Spirit.

Genesis 1:1–2

1 Samuel 16:13

Luke 1:35

Matthew 3:16

John 20:22

Acts 2:3–4

The Descent of the Holy Spirit

Compare the Apostles before and after the descent of the Holy Spirit.

Before Pentecost	After Pentecost

1. What did Jesus tell the Apostles to do in Luke 24:49?

2. What would the Holy Spirit do?

3. What did the Holy Spirit give the Apostles the desire to do?

Name:_____

I Believe in the Holy Spirit

Answer the following questions in complete sentences.

1. Who is the Holy Spirit?

2. Is he God?

3. Is he equal with the Father and the Son?

4. Is the Holy Spirit a Person in the Blessed Trinity? Which Person?

5. How is the Holy Spirit represented?

6. What is the Holy Spirit?

7. Who sends us the Holy Spirit?

8. When do we receive the Holy Spirit?

9. What does it mean to be a "temple of the Holy Spirit"?

10. What are some titles for the Holy Spirit?

Name:_____

Pentecost

Answer the following questions in complete sentences.

1. How long did the Apostles and the other followers of Jesus stay indoors, praying constantly?

2. What happened on the tenth day?

3. How did the Holy Spirit appear?

4. What gifts had the Holy Spirit given the Apostles?

5. How could others receive the grace of salvation and the gifts of the Holy Spirit?

Name:_____

You are Peter

Answer the following questions in complete sentences.

1. Who founded the Church?

2. How was the Church founded?

3. How did Jesus prepare the Apostles?

4. What powers did Jesus give to his Apostles?

5. What are the words of Jesus to Peter in Matthew 16:18–19?

Look up the following Scripture passages and then write a paragraph describing Saint Peter: Mark 1:16–17, Mark 9:5, Matthew 26:34–35, Mark 14:37–38, John 21:17, and Acts 2:38.

The Ascension

Answer the following questions in complete sentences.

1. What is the Mystical Body of Christ?

2. How do we join the Mystical Body of Christ?

3. Who is the head? Who is the soul?

4. What about the rest of us? What part of the Mystical Body of Christ are we?

5. What role do you have in the Mystical Body of Christ?

Write out 1 Corinthians 12:13–21.

Name:_____

The One True Church

Answer the following questions in complete sentences. You might need to ask your teacher for help when answering these questions.

1. How do you know you belong to the true Church of Jesus Christ?

2. How do you know your Church is free from error?

3. What if you do not want to go to church and instead read the Bible. Is that enough?

4. Why is the Catholic Church the true Church?

5. Some Christian religions accept only what is in the Bible, but Catholics accept Sacred Tradition too. Why is it necessary to have Tradition as well as the Bible? Read 2 Thessalonians 2:15.

6. Some churches do not have Confession and instead only pray to God for forgiveness. Why would you tell someone that Confession is better?

7. How would you explain to someone the truth that Jesus is really and truly present in the Eucharist?

Name:_____

Christ's Church

Draw pictures and describe each of the following.

The Church Triumphant

The Church Suffering

The Church Militant

Name:_____

The Identity of the Church

In Scripture we are given many images to help us understand what the Church is. The Church is often described as a sheepfold, a vineyard, and the Bride of Christ. The Scripture passages listed below use the image of a building for the Church. After reading each passage, tell what we learn about the Church from this image.

Matthew 21:42

Acts 4:11

1 Corinthians 3:9–17

Ephesians 2:19–22

1 Peter 2:4–8

Name:_____

Eastern and Western Rites

Answer the following questions in complete sentences.

1. The Eastern and Western rites differ in the way they practice the Faith. Explain the differences between the Eastern and Western rites.

2. From your class discussion, list some of the Eastern rites of the Catholic Church.

3. Are the Eastern and Western rites united in what they believe?

4. Have you ever attended an Eastern rite liturgy? If so, describe your experience.

Name:_____

Four Marks of the Church

Write about each of the four marks of the Church.

one

holy

catholic

apostolic

Name:_____

Symbols of the Church

Explain these different symbols of the Church.

Mystical Body of Christ

Sheepfold

Vineyard

Bark (ship)

Mother

Church Militant

Bride of Christ

Faith and Life Series • Grade 5 • Chapter 25 • Lesson 4

Name:_____

The Church Rules

Answer the following questions in complete sentences.

1. How is the Church divine?

2. How is the Church human?

3. Has the Church always been able to work together in perfect agreement? Give two examples from the early Church.

4. To whom did Jesus give the power to govern the Church?

5. Who guided them in their decisions?

Name:_____

Bishops, Priests, and Deacons

Answer the following questions in complete sentences.

1. Who were the first bishops?

2. Where did your bishop receive his powers?

3. What does a bishop do and where does he do it?

4. What do priests do? Where do they serve the Church?

5. What do deacons do?

Name:_____

The Pope

Answer the following questions in complete sentences.

1. Who did Jesus institute as the first Pope?

2. What happens in Matthew 16:18–19?

3. What happens in John 21:15–17?

4. Who is the Pope today?

5. How did he become Pope?

6. What does "successor of Peter" mean?

Name:_____

The Precepts of the Church

Answer the following questions in complete sentences.

1. What does it mean to assist at Mass on all Sundays and Holy Days of Obligation?

2. Why must we go to Mass on Sundays and not another day of the week?

4. On what days must we fast and abstain?

5. What is the eucharistic fast?

6. How often must we confess our sins?

7. How often must we receive Holy Communion?

8. During what part of the year must we receive Holy Communion?

9. How must we contribute to the support of the Church?

Name:_____

The Holy Spirit in the Church

Answer the following questions in complete sentences.

1. How has the Church kept her teachings free from error?

2. What is the Church's mission?

3. How has the Holy Spirit assisted the Church in her mission?

4. Who has the power to interpret Sacred Scripture and Sacred Tradition?

5. Who has this power now? How was it passed on?

Name:_____

Sacred Scripture & Sacred Tradition

Answer the following questions in complete sentences.

1. Who has the authority to interpret Sacred Scripture?

2. What is Sacred Scripture?

3. Who decided what books would make up the Bible?

4. What is Sacred Tradition?

5. From where did the Apostles receive their teaching?

6. Who interprets Sacred Tradition?

7. Who inspires them to interpret Sacred Tradition?

Infallibility

Answer the following questions in complete sentences.

1. What is infallibility?

2. Who has the charism of infallibility?

3. What teachings are protected infallibly?

4. Must we believe and accept teachings that are infallible? Why?

5. What is an ecumenical council?

6. When was the last ecumenical council? What was it called?

7. What does "Where Peter is, there too is the Church" mean?

8. What do the Pope and the bishops united with him constitute?

9. Can the Church be incorrect in her teaching the truths revealed by God?

10. Can the Pope alone be incorrect in teaching the truths revealed by God?

Name:_____

Evangelization

Answer the following questions in complete sentences.

1. Why does the Church try to teach all nations?

2. Who are missionaries?

3. What do missionaries do?

4. Does evangelization always have to occur far away?

5. Who needs evangelization?

6. How can you help the missions?

7. How can you evangelize?

Name:_____

Child of God

Reflect on the following statements as both a child of your parents and a child of God.

1. Did they/God give you life?

2. Did they/God care for your body?

3. Did they/God care for your soul?

4. Did they/God raise you well?

5. Did they/God give you gifts out of love?

6. Did they/God punish you in order to correct you?

7. Did they/God unite you to God?

8. Did they/God give you grace?

9. Did they/God teach you about the Sacraments?

10. Were you obedient?

11. Were you faithful?

12. Are they/God your Savior?

Name:_____

Sacraments

Compare the natural and the supernatural and describe the supernatural effects of the Sacraments.

Natural	*Supernatural*
1. Water/baths:	1. Baptism:
washes clean and gives life	
2. Forgiveness:	2. Penance:
reunites people	
we are sorry for our mistakes	
3. Bread and wine:	3. Eucharist:
nourish the body	
quench our thirst	
4. Adulthood:	4. Confirmation:
responsible for our own life	
make our own decision	
receive new freedoms	
5. Marriage:	5. Matrimony:
husband and wife share love	
husband and wife have children	
husband and wife are faithful	
6. Priesthood:	6. Holy Orders:
man works for God	
man gives himself to the Church	
man celebrates the Sacraments	
7. Medicine:	7. Anointing of the Sick:
doctor comes to see you	
you are made well again	
you become stronger	

Name:_____

Caring for Our Souls

Answer the following questions in complete sentences.

1. Why does the Church have Sacraments?

2. What does "to sanctify" mean?

3. What does Baptism do for us?

4. If we are baptized, why do we still sin?

5. Why do we need the Sacrament of Penance?

6. What are the two kinds of sin?

7. What are the two kinds of actual sin? Can you commit an actual sin accidentally?

8. What three things are needed in order for a sin to be mortal?

9. What are the five steps to a good Confession?

10. How are your sins forgiven? By whom and by what power?

Name:_____

Called to Holiness

Jesus gave the Church seven Sacraments to restore God's life of grace to souls. See if you can find all seven Sacraments in the puzzle below. Some of the Sacraments consist of more than one word.

```
G  T  A  C  E  F  K  N  O  T  H  S  D  I  O  C  E  S  E
R  A  N  O  S  A  V  I  O  R  T  H  W  C  H  O  M  E  N
A  B  I  S  H  O  P  V  N  I  F  O  M  X  C  N  I  O  N
C  A  A  T  O  L  N  D  Y  P  A  R  I  S  H  F  A  L  T
I  P  A  R  T  E  X  I  S  T  I  F  R  I  E  I  N  D  S
O  T  E  U  C  H  A  R  I  S  T  R  Y  Z  P  R  A  Y  E
U  I  U  A  N  O  O  L  S  B  H  I  Q  U  E  M  A  S  T
S  S  C  A  P  P  O  L  I  N  G  S  U  L  J  A  S  I  A
A  M  H  P  E  E  K  L  Y  O  S  T  R  A  N  T  O  C  K
A  N  O  I  N  T  I  N  G  O  F  T  H  E  S  I  C  K  E
J  A  R  N  A  M  A  M  B  L  R  O  U  N  D  O  D  Y  P
S  T  I  N  N  I  N  G  F  X  C  D  E  A  C  N  O  L  E
I  O  T  Y  C  O  M  M  U  N  I  T  E  J  O  U  R  N  D
S  A  S  A  E  R  A  M  E  N  M  A  T  R  I  M  O  N  Y
A  L  S  A  C  R  E  D  I  N  E  R  E  Y  S  W  X  L  S
```

List the seven Sacraments.

1.

2.

3.

4.

5.

6.

7.

Name:_____

Behold Your Mother

Read John 19:26–27. Answer the following questions in complete sentences.

1. Who was at the Cross with Jesus?

2. To whom did Jesus give his Mother?

3. Who does he represent?

4. What titles do we give Mary today?

5. How is Mary a good model for us?

6. Will Mary pray for us?

The Assumption

Answer the following questions in complete sentences.

1. What is the Assumption?

2. Why was Mary assumed into heaven with both her body and her soul?

3. When do we celebrate the Assumption every year?

4. Does Mary continue to be our Mother in heaven?

5. Is Mary a saint?

6. Why is Mary the holiest of all saints?

Name:_____

Mary Intercedes for Us

Answer the following questions in complete sentences.

1. Why did Jesus perform a miracle at the wedding feast of Cana?

2. Who asked him to perform this miracle?

3. What did he do?

4. To whom was Mary being motherly?

5. Read John 2:5. What is Mary's advice for us?

6. What effect did this have on Jesus' Apostles? Read John 2:11 for the answer.

Name:_____

The Mother of God in Our Lives

The following are some of the feasts we celebrate in honor of Mary. Tell what each feast commemorates and find out the date on which each is celebrated.

Annunciation:

Assumption:

Queenship of Mary:

Immaculate Conception:

Solemnity of Mary, Mother of God:

Visitation:

Birth of Mary:

Our Lady of Guadalupe:

Presentation of the Blessed Virgin Mary:

Our Lady of Lourdes:

Our Lady of Mount Carmel:

Our Lady of the Rosary:

Immaculate Heart of Mary:

Name:_____

Death

Answer the following questions in complete sentences.

1. Will we all die someday?

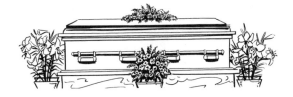

2. Should we fear death?

3. Will our bodies rise? Will our souls die?

4. What happens when we die? Will Jesus judge us?

5. What will we be judged upon?

6. Where will your soul go if you die in a state of mortal sin without repentance?

7. Where will your soul go if you die in perfect grace without stain of sin?

8. Where will your soul go if you die in grace but are still in need of purification?

9. Will souls who go to purgatory someday go to heaven?

Name:_____

Eternal Life

Answer the following questions in complete sentences.

1. What will happen if we die in a state of grace?

2. What is heaven like?

3. What keeps us forever happy in heaven?

4. Will we miss earth?

5. Will we forget others in heaven?

6. Who will we meet in heaven?

7. What is the best part of heaven?

Name:_____

Unto Everlasting Life

Fill in the crossword puzzle with the correct words.

Across

1. "_____ life is this: to know you, the only true God, and him whom you have sent, Jesus Christ" (John 17:3).
2. Because of the _____ of the body our souls will be reunited with our bodies.
4. The second _____ of Jesus will be at the end of the world.

Down

3. The worst suffering of the souls in _____ is the eternal loss of God.
5. _____ is not the end of our existence.
6. Souls are purified in _____ before they live forever with God.
7. At the end of the world there will be a _____ judgment in which all men will be judged.
8. At the moment of our death we will each have a _____ judgment.
9. _____ is our true home.

All of us are called to be saints in heaven. Name one thing you can do every day to help you on your way to heaven.

Name:_____

Second Coming

Describe the Second Coming in a short paragraph.